FINANCIAL CRIMES ENFORCEMENT NETWORK
Annual Report
Fiscal Year 2004

Message to Stakeholders

In December 2003, I was honored to be appointed the fourth Director of the Financial Crimes Enforcement Network. From my previous positions at the Department of the Treasury, I already greatly appreciated the front-line role that this organization plays in the war against terrorist financing, money laundering, and other financial crimes by virtue of its role as administrator of the Bank Secrecy Act.

As I came to know the organization, I was delighted to find a community of highly motivated and skilled employees dedicated to our mission. However, I also found an organization facing significant challenges. For example:

- *The structure for administering the Bank Secrecy Act is uniquely fragmented.* The Secretary of the Treasury has delegated responsibility for administering this important law to the Financial Crimes Enforcement Network. However, we must depend on a variety of other organizations to fulfill various aspects of this task, including collecting the Bank Secrecy Act data and examining covered institutions for compliance with the law.

- *Less than optimum use was being made of our relatively scant resources.* The single largest job title within the Financial Crimes Enforcement Network is Intelligence Research Specialist. Yet many of these skilled analysts were performing relatively simple database queries in direct support of our law enforcement customers. This is important research that needs to be done, but law enforcement agencies could more efficiently perform these queries themselves if they had direct and user-friendly access to the Bank Secrecy Act data.

- *The organizational structure was top-heavy and functions were not well aligned with our mission.* For example, when I took this job, we had 41 managers and 199 nonsupervisory employees, a ratio of one manager to less than five employees. In addition, operations were "stovepiped" and several tasks were being unnecessarily duplicated in different parts of the organization.

This report describes steps we have taken this year to address these challenges. For example, we have:

- Realigned our organization to reflect our functional priorities, reduced the number of managers to 26, and enhanced our processes for overseeing and assisting our regulatory partners to whom compliance examination responsibilities for the Bank Secrecy Act have been delegated.

- Begun to better use our skilled professionals for complex analysis of financial intelligence, including classified data.

- Launched a major initiative to make Bank Secrecy Act data and analytical tools available to authorized users through an easy-to-use, secure, web-based program. This initiative, called BSA Direct, will help to assure that we can continue the needs of our law enforcement customers for financial data as our employees move toward more complex analysis. This initiative will also provide the architecture for greatly expanding e-filing of Bank Secrecy Act data.

- Taken steps to enhance data exchanges with the financial institutions that file Bank Secrecy Act reports, with our regulatory partners, with law enforcement agencies that use that information to track financial crimes, with the intelligence community, and with our counterpart government agencies, known as financial intelligence units, across the globe.

I look forward to building on these accomplishments and to seeing the fruits of these actions in the years ahead.

William J. Fox
Director
January 2005

Contents

About the
Financial Crimes Enforcement Network

The Financial Crimes Enforcement Network, a bureau within the Department of the Treasury, is America's financial intelligence unit. Our mission is to safeguard the financial system from the abuses of terrorist financing, money laundering and other financial crime.

We fulfill this mission through our role as administrator of the Bank Secrecy Act, as amended. Among a broad range of interrelated activities, we:

- Issue, interpret, and enforce compliance with regulations implementing the Bank Secrecy Act, which includes key provisions of Title III of the USA PATRIOT Act;

- Support and oversee compliance examination functions delegated to other federal regulators;

- Manage the collection, processing, storage, and dissemination of Bank Secrecy Act data;

- Maintain a government-wide access service to the Bank Secrecy Act data, and network users with overlapping interests;

- Conduct analysis in support of policy makers; law enforcement, regulatory, and intelligence agencies; and the financial industry.

Because illicit financial activity is not confined to our borders, we also work to build global cooperation, strengthen other countries' efforts to deter and detect financial crime, and share information with a wide range of countries. These actions include coordinating with and collaborating on anti-terrorism and anti-money laundering initiatives with our financial intelligence unit counterparts around the world.

To learn more about the Financial Crimes Enforcement Network, visit our website at **www.fincen.gov**.

Mission Statement

The mission of the Financial Crimes Enforcement Network is to safeguard the financial system from the abuses of financial crime, including terrorist financing, money laundering, and other illicit activity.

We achieve this mission by:

Administering *the Bank Secrecy Act;*

Supporting *law enforcement, intelligence, and regulatory agencies through sharing and analysis of financial intelligence;*

Building *global cooperation with our counterpart financial intelligence units;*

Networking *people, ideas, and information.*

History

The U.S. Department of the Treasury established the Financial Crimes Enforcement Network in 1990 to provide a government-wide multi-source financial intelligence and analysis network. The organization's operation was broadened in 1994 to include regulatory responsibilities for administering the Bank Secrecy Act, one of the nation's most potent weapons for preventing corruption of the U.S. financial system.

The Bank Secrecy Act, enacted in 1970, authorizes the Secretary of the Treasury to issue regulations requiring that financial institutions keep records and file reports on certain financial transactions determined to have a high degree of usefulness in criminal, tax, regulatory investigations and proceedings, and certain intelligence and counter-terrorism matters. The authority of the Secretary to administer Title II of the Bank Secrecy Act (codified at 31 U.S.C. 5311-5330 with implementing regulations at 31 C.F.R. Part 103) has been delegated to the Director of the Financial Crimes Enforcement Network.

Hundreds of thousands of financial institutions are subject to Bank Secrecy Act reporting and recordkeeping requirements. These include depository institutions (e.g., banks, credit unions and thrifts); brokers or dealers in securities; money services businesses (e.g., money transmitters; issuers, redeemers and sellers of money orders and travelers' checks; check cashers and currency exchangers); and casinos and card clubs.

The USA PATRIOT Act of 2001, enacted shortly after the 9/11 attacks in America, broadened the scope of the Bank Secrecy Act to focus on terrorist financing as well as money laundering. The Act also gave the Financial Crimes Enforcement Network additional responsibilities and authorities in both important areas, and established the organization as a bureau within the Treasury Department.

On March 8, 2004, the organization became a part of the Department of the Treasury's new Office of Terrorism and Financial Intelligence. This is the lead office in the Treasury Department for fighting the financial war on terror, combating financial crime, and enforcing economic sanctions against rogue nations.

Overview
of Money Laundering & Illicit Financing

Money laundering is the effort to take cash derived from an illicit activity, often in large sums, and "clean" it through a series of financial transactions that disguise its origins and make it appear to be a legitimate part of the financial system. Illicit financing, including funding of terrorist activity, often involves "reverse money laundering"–the movement of "clean" money to support criminal purposes.

Detecting and combating these two types of activities requires different approaches and tools. With money laundering, investigators and analysts essentially need to look through a telescope to watch the movement of large amounts of "dirty" cash. With terrorist financing, they need a microscope to see the movement of funds–often very small amounts of "clean" money–by people attempting an evil purpose.

In FY 2004, the Financial Crimes Enforcement Network enhanced its efforts to detect and prevent both types of illegal activity. While continuing to collect and analyze Bank Secrecy Act and other financial data, we have stepped up our efforts to identify threats and to exchange information with the financial industry, law enforcement agencies, financial intelligence units in other countries, and the intelligence community.

Al Qaeda funded the hijackers in the United States by three primary and unexceptional means: (1) wire transfers from overseas to the United States, (2) the physical transport of cash or traveler's checks into the United States, and (3) the accessing of funds held in foreign financial institutions by debit or credit cards. Once here, all of the hijackers used the U.S. banking system to store their funds and facilitate their transactions.

–9/11 Commission, Terrorist Financing Staff Monograph, August 21, 2004

Bank Secrecy Act Reporting in Fiscal Year 2004

The Bank Secrecy Act is the nation's first and most comprehensive federal anti-money laundering statute. Since it was enacted in 1970, the Act has been amended several times to improve and enhance information collection. The Bank Secrecy Act authorizes the Secretary of the Treasury to issue regulations requiring banks and other financial institutions to take a number of precautions against financial crime, including filing reports that have been determined to have a high degree of usefulness in criminal, tax, regulatory investigations and proceedings, and certain intelligence and counter-terrorism matters.

The Bank Secrecy Act's record keeping and reporting requirements help to create a financial trail that law enforcement and intelligence agencies can use to track criminals, their activities, and their assets. Reports required under the Bank Secrecy Act include:

- Currency Transaction Reports, which describe cash transactions exceeding $10,000. More than 13 million Currency Transaction Reports are filed each year. Currency transaction reporting requirements are a key impediment to criminal attempts to legitimize the proceeds of crime.

- Suspicious Activity Reports, which describe financial transactions of any amount and type that financial institutions suspect may be related to illicit activity. These reports are especially valuable to law enforcement and intelligence agencies because they reflect activity considered problematic or unusual by financial institutions. Because these reports are based on suspicions, rather than facts, and because they contain sensitive personal information, Suspicious Activity Reports may be disclosed and disseminated only under strict guidelines. Unauthorized disclosure of Suspicious Activity Reports is a violation of criminal law.

- Several other reports of financial transactions, money services business registrations, and designations of entities exempt from Currency Transaction Report requirements.

The number of Bank Secrecy Act reports filed in Fiscal Year 2004 was substantially higher than the number filed the previous year:

- The total number of Bank Secrecy Act reports filed grew by more than 646,000, from 14.2 million in Fiscal Year 2003 to 14.8 million in Fiscal Year 2004.

■ The number of Suspicious Activity Reports grew by more than 250,000, to a total of 663,655.

The Financial Crimes Enforcement Network encourages electronic filing of Bank Secrecy Act reports as a way to speed up the secure flow of information from financial institution filers to law enforcement and regulatory agencies. In Fiscal Year 2004, about 11% of Bank Secrecy Act reports were e-filed, almost three times the 4% e-filed in Fiscal Year 2003.

See Appendix A for the list of Bank Secrecy Act reports and the number filed in Fiscal Years 2003 and 2004.

The electronic system for the filing of Bank Secrecy Act (BSA) information processed its two millionth form on August 25. It took 500 days in operation to receive the first million and less than 200 days to receive the second million. We anticipate the three million mark will occur in less than 100 days. Approximately 40,000 forms are filed electronically each week. FinCEN expects that the numbers will increase substantially as FinCEN implements new system architecture.

–Financial Crimes Enforcement Network Weekly Activities Report, September 2, 2004

Highlights of Operations by Major Operating Unit

The Financial Crimes Enforcement Network is organized into the Office of the Director and four major operating divisions. The four divisions cover regulatory activity, analysis, client liaison and services, and administration and communications. In addition, the Office of Chief Counsel provides legal services to all these units. An organization chart appears in Appendix B. The following pages list key accomplishments of each major operating unit in Fiscal Year 2004 and priorities for Fiscal Year 2005.

"I feel that my job is clear: To lead the Financial Crimes Enforcement Network to become the gold standard in collecting, understanding, analyzing, employing, and disseminating financial information to combat terrorism & financial crime."

–William J. Fox, Director,
Financial Crimes Enforcement Network, June 16, 2004

1. Office of the Director

The Office of the Director consists of the Director, Deputy Director, Chief of Staff, Office of Security, and Office of Outreach and Workplace Solutions.

Major Accomplishments in Fiscal Year 2004

- Restructured the organization to align the Financial Crimes Enforcement Network's functional units with our strategic priorities. An organization chart appears in Appendix B. Following the restructuring, we recruited and selected four executive-level managers, the Associate Directors for our Regulatory Policy and Programs, Analytic, Client Liaison and Services, and Administration and Communications Divisions. (See biographies in Appendix C.) Among other changes, the realignment:

  - Set up a new Office of Compliance with responsibility for assuring that examinations for compliance with the Bank Secrecy Act and related requirements are uniform and effective.

  - Brought together a variety of tasks related to managing the Bank Secrecy Act data; the systems required to store, collect, and disseminate the data; and activities to interact with the customers who use that data and other services that we provide.

  - Expanded the Equal Opportunity and Diversity Office into the Office of Workplace Solutions, which has new responsibilities for establishing a conflict management program outside the equal employment opportunity area, coordinating responsibilities for assuring that we are meeting accessibility standards under Section 508 of the Rehabilitation Act, and setting up new outreach, recruitment, and student programs.

  - Reduced the number of managers from 41 to 26, bringing the ratio of supervisors to nonsupervisory employees more in line with the needs of our professional work force.

  - Established a new training function charged with developing career path progressions for all employees.

- Imposed special measures authorized by Section 311 of the USA PATRIOT Act against one foreign jurisdiction and two foreign financial institutions designated as being of primary money laundering concern.

- Began moving the Financial Crimes Enforcement Network from a security posture emphasizing "public trust" to one emphasizing "national security" in order to ensure our analysts greater access to classified information crucial to anti-terrorism efforts. This ongoing effort includes upgrading employee background investigation and security clearance requirements, tightening physical security, and upgrading computer security.

- Led the U.S. delegation to the 12th Egmont Group Plenary held in Guernsey. The Egmont Group is a network of 94 financial intelligence units from around the globe. During this meeting, membership status was extended to 10 new financial intelligence units: Belize, Cook Islands, Egypt, Georgia, Gibraltar, Grenada, Indonesia, Macedonia, St. Kitts and Nevis, and Ukraine.

- Spoke before a wide variety of industry and government groups, both here and abroad, and testified before committees and subcommittees of the U.S. Senate and House of Representatives.

Priorities for Fiscal Year 2005

- Complete the organizational alignment, to include filling ten remaining senior management positions being held by persons serving in an acting capacity.

- Continue to build the security infrastructure, technology infrastructure, employee skills, and methodologies needed to detect and combat terrorist financing as well as other financial crime.

- Publish a revised strategic plan that better reflects our role as a regulatory agency, our increasing role in combating terrorist financing, and our long-range vision for providing law enforcement and regulatory agencies with better access to the Bank Secrecy Act data while supporting these agencies with more complex and sophisticated analyses.

- Effectively steward our increasing budget by applying additional resources to priority areas, including strengthening our regulatory function, improving our analysts' ability to perform complex analyses with all-source data, improving our organizational infrastructure, and enhancing e-government capabilities.

- Attract, develop, and retain a high-performing, diverse workforce through implementation of a new recruitment program, adopting recruitment and hiring flexibilities, and using effective performance management and individual development plans.

- Improve both lateral and vertical communications within the organization.

- Enhance collaboration within Treasury's Office of Terrorism and Financial Intelligence through joint projects with the Office of Foreign Assets Control and the Office of Intelligence and Analysis.

2. Regulatory Policy & Programs Division

The Regulatory Policy and Programs Division conducts a broad range of activities related to the administration of the Bank Secrecy Act, as amended by the USA PATRIOT Act of 2001. For example, we develop and implement appropriate anti-money laundering program, recordkeeping, and reporting regulations for vulnerable sectors of the financial industry. While responsibility for examining financial institutions for compliance with Bank Secrecy Act regulations has been delegated to other federal agencies, * the Regulatory Policy and Programs Division provides support for and oversight over the examination functions to help ensure effective and uniform application of the regulations.

The Financial Crimes Enforcement Network works closely with these regulatory partners, which refer to us cases of noncompliance with Bank Secrecy Act regulations. When warranted, we impose civil money penalties or lesser enforcement remedies against violating institutions as a way to promote and encourage greater compliance.

*A variety of self-regulatory organizations and state regulatory authorities also conduct Bank Secrecy Act examination activities for their own purposes.

Federal Regulatory Partners

Federal Deposit Insurance Corporation

Board of Governors of the Federal Reserve

Office of the Comptroller of the Currency
(Department of the Treasury)

Internal Revenue Service, Small Business/Self-Employed Division
(Department of the Treasury)

Office of Thrift Supervision (Department of the Treasury)

National Credit Union Administration

Securities and Exchange Commission

Commodity Futures Trading Commission

We also take special measures authorized under Section 311 of the USA PATRIOT Act of 2001 if the Secretary of the Treasury finds reasonable grounds for concluding that a jurisdiction or financial institution is of primary money laundering concern. Under this authority, we are authorized to impose a range of special measures that require U.S. financial institutions to take a variety of remedial measures, including terminating accounts involving a jurisdiction or financial institution determined to be of primary money laundering concern.

```
FOR IMMEDIATE RELEASE
     May 13, 2004
```

FinCEN Assesses $25 Million Civil Money Penalty Against Riggs Bank N.A.

The Financial Crimes Enforcement Network (FinCEN) announced today that Riggs Bank N.A. consented to the assessment of the largest civil monetary penalty ever brought against a U.S. financial institution for violations under the Bank Secrecy Act (BSA), the statute requiring financial institutions to guard against money laundering. The $25 million civil money penalty was brought against Riggs Bank N.A. for willful, systemic violations of the anti-money laundering program and suspicious activity and currency transaction reporting requirements of the BSA.

FinCEN determined that Riggs failed to design and implement an anti-money laundering program tailored to the risks of its business that would have ensured appropriate and timely reporting of suspicious conduct.

"Riggs' failure to implement an adequate antimoney laundering program resulted in the failure to file timely, accurate and complete Bank Secrecy Act reports. The facts of this case demonstrate Riggs' systemic failure to comply with its obligations under the Bank Secrecy Act," said William J. Fox, Director of FinCEN. "The Riggs failure is by no means emblematic of the financial industry as a whole, which functions well in complying with its anti-money laundering reporting requirements. These reports are critical to the U.S. government's efforts to thwart financiers of terror and other criminals and the financial community should be commended for the valuable contribution it has made to these efforts."

The penalty assessment is concurrent with the $25 million penalty also assessed against Riggs by The Office of the Comptroller of the Currency. The penalties will be satisfied by one payment of $25 million to the Department of the Treasury.

Major Accomplishments in Fiscal Year 2004

- Established an Office of Compliance to support and communicate with regulatory agencies that examine financial institutions for Bank Secrecy Act compliance.

- Negotiated agreements with the five federal banking regulatory agencies to routinely exchange information about Bank Secrecy Act examination activities, including the identification of financial institutions with significant Bank Secrecy Act compliance deficiencies.

- Participated in the drafting of revised Bank Secrecy Act examination procedures with the five Federal banking agencies.

- Became a participating member of the federal Financial Institutions Examination Council's Bank Secrecy Act/Anti-Money Laundering Working Group, which is responsible for strengthening communications among the Federal banking agencies and FinCEN, ensuring consistency in examination policies and procedures, and coordinating examiner training.

- Assessed civil money penalties on two institutions, $25 million on Riggs Bank, NA and $10,000 on Hartsfield Capital Securities, Inc., for willful violations of the Bank Secrecy Act.

- Extended Suspicious Activity Reporting requirements to the futures commission merchant and introducing broker industries.

- Continued to support, staff, and develop the expansion of the Bank Secrecy Act Advisory Group, which includes 48 members representing industry, regulatory agencies and law enforcement. (See more about the Bank Secrecy Act Advisory Group on page 19.)

- Imposed special measures authorized by Section 311 of the USA PATRIOT Act against one jurisdiction (Burma) and two financial institutions (Burmese financial institutions Myanmar Mayflower Bank and Asia Wealth Bank).

- Proposed special measures authorized by Section 311 against another three financial institutions (Commercial Bank of Syria, First Merchant Bank OSH Ltd., and Infobank) designated as being of primary money laundering concern.

For additional workload data, see Appendix D, Table D-1.

Priorities for Fiscal Year 2005

- Finalize agreements with the Commodity Futures Trading Commission, the Internal Revenue Service, and the Securities Exchange Commission to routinely exchange information about Bank Secrecy Act examination activities, including the identification of financial institutions with significant Bank Secrecy Act compliance deficiencies.

- Negotiate information exchange agreements with the various state supervisory agencies that examine for compliance with the Bank Secrecy Act or similar state regulations.

- Develop a system for securely managing the information flow resulting from the information exchange agreements with Federal banking regulators and state supervisory agencies, and develop initial reports on financial industry compliance based on the information provided.

- Enhance processes for identifying financial institutions with Bank Secrecy Act compliance issues, such as chronic errors in Suspicious Activity Reports, and take appropriate action, either alone or in conjunction with the federal agency with authority over the financial institution.

- Continue to enforce the Bank Secrecy Act through the assessment of civil remedies where appropriate, including the assessment of civil money penalties in cases involving willful violations of the Bank Secrecy Act, and work to close enforcement case matters more expeditiously.

- Expand the human resources in the Division so that we may better fulfill our original regulatory function, as well as serve and assist our regulatory partners.

"There must be a unifying center to our anti-money laundering efforts. Mr. Fox's recent proposals to strengthen FinCEN's role in BSA compliance… are important steps in that direction."

–U.S. Representative Sue Kelly, Vice-Chair, House Financial Services Committee, and Chair, Subcommittee on Oversight and Investigations, June 16, 2004

- Finalize pending Bank Secrecy Act regulations, including:
    - Regulations that would require investment advisers, commodity trading advisors, insurance companies, unregistered investment companies, and dealers in precious metals, stones or jewels to establish anti-money laundering programs;
    - Regulations that would impose a Suspicious Activity Report filing requirement for insurance companies and mutual funds; and
    - A final rule implementing Section 312 of the USA PATRIOT Act regarding special due diligence for correspondent accounts and private banking accounts.

- Issue proposed regulations that would require loan or finance companies to establish an anti-money laundering program, and determine whether it is appropriate to issue proposed regulations that would require persons involved in real estate closings and settlements, businesses engaged in vehicle sales, and travel agencies to establish such programs.

- Review on an ongoing basis the effectiveness of Bank Secrecy Act regulations already implemented.

- Issue a redesigned, simplified Suspicious Activity Report form for money services businesses to provide better data for analytic and law enforcement purposes, while reducing the preparation burden for money services businesses and lowering the processing costs for the government.

- Continue to provide clear, timely guidance to regulated industries to position them to meet their compliance obligations under the Bank Secrecy Act.

- Establish mechanisms for providing feedback to regulated industries regarding the usefulness of Bank Secrecy Act data collected.

- Enhance the quality of Suspicious Activity Report data by emphasizing their importance in training seminars and presentations to the regulated industries, and monitoring filed Suspicious Activity Reports to minimize the occurrence of blank or incomplete data fields.

■ Reinvigorate our efforts to regulate money services businesses through a variety of strategies, including expanding efforts to identify the universe of such businesses and to uncover underground money services businesses and other informal value transfer systems.

Bank Secrecy Act Advisory Group

Congress established the Bank Secrecy Act Advisory Group in 1992 to enable the financial services industry and law enforcement to advise the Secretary of the Treasury on ways to enhance the utility of Bank Secrecy Act reports. Since 1994, the Advisory Group has served as a forum for industry, regulators and law enforcement to communicate about how Suspicious Activity Reports and other Bank Secrecy Act reports are used by law enforcement and how the reporting requirements can be improved. Members from the private sector, financial institutions and trade groups participate. The Director of the Financial Crimes Enforcement Network chairs the Group.

The Advisory Group, which is not subject to the Federal Advisory Committee Act, meets twice each year, usually in May and October, in Washington, DC. In light of the expansion of Bank Secrecy Act reporting requirements, especially since the enactment of the USA PATRIOT Act of 2001, the Financial Crimes Enforcement Network is currently reconstituting the Advisory Group to ensure that it fully and fairly reflects the entire Bank Secrecy Act constituency. The Advisory Group now has 48 members.

The Advisory Group utilizes a variety of permanent and ad hoc subcommittees to identify and analyze relevant issues. Current subcommittees focus on: Suspicious Activity Report issues; Bank Secrecy Act examination consistency; unauthorized disclosure of Suspicious Activity Reports; wire transfer/customer identification rules; and reducing the filing of Currency Transaction Reports with little or no value to law enforcement. The Advisory Group also co-chairs publication of The SAR Activity Review, which in August 2004 became *The SAR Activity Review—Trends, Tips & Issues*. This publication provides meaningful information to the financial community about the preparation, use, and value of Suspicious Activity Reports.

Following unauthorized press reports concerning Suspicious Activity Reports, the Advisory Group also issued a statement explaining why the confidentiality of these reports must be strictly maintained.

The unauthorized disclosure of Suspicious Activity Reports is not only a violation of federal criminal law, but it undermines the very purpose for which the suspicious activity reporting system was created - the protection of our financial system through the prevention, detection, and prosecution of financial crimes and terrorist financing. The unauthorized disclosure of Suspicious Activity Reports can compromise the national security of the United States as well as threaten the safety and security of those institutions and individuals who file such reports. The Bank Secrecy Act Advisory Group is committed to continuing to work with the Financial Crimes Enforcement Network, the federal functional regulatory agencies, law enforcement, and the financial services industry to ensure that the information contained in Suspicious Activity Reports is safeguarded, and that anyone who makes an intentional, unauthorized disclosure of a Suspicious Activity Report is brought to justice, whether that person is inside or outside of the Government.

–Statement by Bank Secrecy Act Advisory Group, August 18, 2004

3. Analytics Division

The Financial Crimes Enforcement Network is the largest overt collector of financial crimes intelligence in the United States. The information we collect is highly valuable in combating terrorism and investigating money laundering and other financial crime. We mine data collected under the Bank Secrecy Act, and link it with law enforcement, commercial, and other intelligence data sources to follow the money trails of terrorists and other criminals and to identify networks of people and accounts engaged in unlawful activity.

Our employees include approximately 100 analysts who analyze the Bank Secrecy Act and other data to provide support for regulatory and policy decisions, to support law enforcement agencies investigating financial crimes, and to support intelligence agencies. We proactively identify individuals and networks whose financial activity is suspicious and refer that information to appropriate law enforcement agencies. Our analysts also develop threat assessments, industry reports, and technical guides to financial transaction mechanisms.

Major Accomplishments in Fiscal Year 2004

- Initiated over 250 referrals to law enforcement agencies based on proactive analysis of Bank Secrecy Act and other data. These referrals included reports identifying activities indicative of terrorist financing, money laundering, and other illicit financial activity.

- Produced 56 strategic analytic products, including seven threat assessments, and 14 country/region or industry reports based on analysis of Suspicious Activity Reports.

- Worked with analysts from other financial intelligence units on major cases with international significance, including the Parmalat financial fraud and the Madrid train bombing investigations.

- Supported over 2,900 investigative efforts through research and analysis of Bank Secrecy Act and other data.

- Analyzed money laundering and illicit financing schemes based on use of commodities, false invoicing, trade diversion, and other mechanisms.

- Researched more than 19,300 subjects being investigated by law enforcement.

For additional workload data, see Appendix D, Table D-2.

Priorities for Fiscal Year 2005

- Improve our abilities to use our data and technology to inform the financial industry of financial transaction activity indicative of possible terrorist funding and financing. Financial institutions have advised us that this is their most pressing need in identifying and reporting terrorism-related activity at the earliest possible stage.

- Develop a national Money Laundering Threat Assessment platform incorporating Bank Secrecy Act data, especially Suspicious Activity Reports, which will track money laundering threats over large geographic areas, identify changing money laundering methodologies over time, and assist law enforcement and other end users in applying resources to areas of greatest threat. The Threat Assessment will be a living document, updated periodically to incorporate new information.

- Develop and implement a strategy for assisting law enforcement agencies now requesting baseline database research from the Financial Crimes Enforcement Network to more efficiently make those queries themselves. We must take this course of action in order to reallocate our analytic resources to more complex work on terrorist financing and complex money laundering investigative support. We will develop criteria for the types of queries we consider to be baseline, notify law enforcement agencies of why this strategy is being developed, assist them in gaining direct access to Bank Secrecy Act data, and inform stakeholders, including U.S. Senate and House of Representatives authorizing and appropriating committees, of the transition plan.

- Expand analytic interaction with the Egmont Group. We plan to engage in joint analytic initiatives with other financial intelligence units interested in undertaking collaborative analytic products that fuse data, especially suspicious or unusual transaction reporting, to identify investigative lead information on global criminal networks and to develop typologies of international money laundering and terrorist financing methodologies.

> *Vigorous efforts to track terrorist financing must remain front and center in U.S. counterterrorism efforts. The government has recognized that information about terrorist money helps us to understand their networks, search them out, and disrupt their operations.*
>
> *–9/11 Commission Report, July 22, 2004*

4. Client Liaison and Services Division

As Administrator of the Bank Secrecy Act, the Financial Crimes Enforcement Network is responsible for managing the Bank Secrecy Act data filed by the regulated industries. The Client Liaison and Services Division, which is headed by our Chief Information Officer, is responsible for managing the Bank Secrecy Act data.

The Division performs a variety of roles related to collection, processing, and dissemination of the Bank Secrecy Act data. It also provides liaison with domestic law enforcement agencies and others who use the data. For example, the Division manages:

- The *Gateway* program, through which law enforcement agencies and regulators can access the Bank Secrecy Act data through a secure web connection. We authorize Gateway users, train them, and monitor their use to ensure that the data, which are considered law enforcement sensitive, are properly used, disseminated, and kept secure.

- The *Platform* program, which enables Federal law enforcement agency representatives to utilize our databases and analytical tools on-site at our facility.

The Division also provides liaison services with our counterpart foreign intelligence units in other countries and with international organizations that set international standards for anti-money laundering and anti-terrorist financing programs. In addition, it provides the technical infrastructure needed for internal operations within the Financial Crimes Enforcement Network.

Bank Secrecy Act Data Services, Liaison, and Systems and Reporting

Major Accomplishments in Fiscal Year 2004

- Awarded a contract to launch BSA Direct, a major initiative that will provide the architecture for long-range plans to collect, process, store, and disseminate Bank Secrecy Act data. The competitive contract–which covers design, development, and deployment of the system, plus 5 option years for secure web hosting, operations and maintenance–was awarded to EDS, a global information technology services company. BSA Direct will establish a data warehouse with integrated query and analysis tools to streamline and enhance processes for storing, accessing, and analyzing data collected under the Bank Secrecy Act by the various customers of FinCEN. The target date for the completion of the initial phase is October 2005. The full value of the contract award, if all options are exercised, is approximately $18.5 million.

- Enhanced our system for e-filing Bank Secrecy Act reports, and promoted e-filing by institutions with the largest filing volumes. As a result, approximately 11% of Bank Secrecy Act reports were e-filed in FY 2004, compared with 4% in FY 2003.

- Authorized, trained, audited, and provided customer assistance to 2,181 Gateway users, nearly double the 1,105 served in Fiscal Year 2003. Ability to serve this customer base was enhanced by an automated inspection initiative, which allowed inspections to rise from 30 in Fiscal Year 2003 to 313 in Fiscal Year 2004. We also developed online training and testing modules as a way to streamline customer training.

- Sent almost 200 law enforcement information requests to more than 35,000 financial institution points of contact through the law enforcement-financial institution information-sharing program authorized under Section 314(a) of the USA PATRIOT Act. The Division also started a project to move the operation and work flow of the Section 314(a) information-sharing program to a secure online environment.

- Achieved 100% Security Certification and Accreditation of identified key information technology systems.

- Upgraded FinCEN's network infrastructure by replacing a third of our servers, workstations, printers, and wireless devices; upgrading six firewalls to high-capacity, higher level of security appliances; and installing a SPAM filtering system.

- Upgraded FinCEN's Continuation of Operations Plan (COOP) site equipment and software. This site would continue to operate in the event of a major disruption to headquarters operations.

For additional workload figures associated with these activities, see Appendix D, Tables D-3 through D-6.

Priorities for Fiscal Year 2005

- Pilot test and revise initial phases of BSA Direct, followed by full production roll out.

- Continue to increase electronic filing of Bank Secrecy Act forms so that at least 40% of the reports filed are filed electronically.

- Develop enterprise-wide architecture for the management of data.

- Pilot test and revise Gateway online training and testing modules.

- Integrate Gateway with BSA Direct.

- Roll out Gateway/BSA Direct online training and testing modules.

- Automate the Gateway networking process, which alerts Gateway users when another law enforcement agency is investigating the same subject or subjects.

- Create an inspection team for Bank Secrecy Act dissemination violation complaints, enhanced collaboration with law enforcement, and quality control of the Gateway program.

- Upgrade and expand FinCEN's network infrastructure.

- Upgrade FinCEN's case and document management capabilities.

- Enhance the law enforcement-financial institution information-sharing program (314 program) by providing participating financial institutions with direct secure web access to requested information and online response capability.

FOR IMMEDIATE RELEASE
    December 17, 2003

Industry Partnership Results in Valuable Investigative Leads
(EXCERPT)

An expedited information-sharing program administered by FinCEN has
yielded numerous productive leads for both terrorist financing and
major money laundering investigations. The program enables federal
law enforcement agencies, through FinCEN, to reach out to over
29,000 financial institutions to locate accounts and transactions of
persons that may be involved in terrorism or money laundering.

The authority to require financial institutions to search recent
account and transaction records and report matches is found in
Section 314(a) of the USA PATRIOT Act of 2001, which requires the
Secretary of the Treasury to adopt regulations governing the sharing
of information about individuals, entities, and organizations
engaged in or reasonably suspected, based on credible evidence,
of engaging in terrorist acts or money laundering activities. The
314(a) system has processed 188 requests submitted by ten federal
agencies from February 18, 2003 to November 25, 2003. These federal
law enforcement organizations have submitted cases in the conduct
of 64 terrorism/terrorist financing cases and 124 money laundering
cases.

Regulations require that law enforcement provide written
certification that subjects submitted to FinCEN are reasonably
suspected based on credible evidence of engaging in terrorist
activity or money laundering. There were 1,256 subjects certified
by law enforcement and forwarded by FinCEN to financial institutions
through the 314(a) system.

The feedback from law enforcement has been overwhelmingly positive
and has resulted in the discovery of hundreds of suspect accounts
and transactions in addition to the issuance of the following:
-407 Grand Jury Subpoenas
-11 Search Warrants
-21 Administrative Subpoenas/Summons
-3 Indictments.

25

Global Activity

The Financial Crimes Enforcement Network is the financial intelligence unit of the United States. We are a member of the Egmont Group of financial intelligence units, an international network of nearly 100 national centers set up specifically to collect information on suspicious or unusual financial activity from the financial industry, to analyze the data, and to make it available to appropriate national authorities and other financial intelligence units for use in combating terrorist funding and other financial crime.

We play a leadership role in the Egmont process, using it as a springboard for improving international cooperation, collaboration, and information sharing. FinCEN's Deputy Director serves as Chair of the Egmont Committee of the Egmont Group, and we participate in all four Egmont Working Groups: Legal, Training/Communications, Outreach, and Operational. In addition, we host the Egmont Secure web, which permits secure online information sharing among Egmont members.

Major Accomplishments in Fiscal Year 2004

- Connected an additional 21 financial intelligence units to the Egmont Secure Web, raising the total connected from 64 in Fiscal Year 2003 to 85 in Fiscal Year 2004.

- Provided regulatory and technical assistance to 27 financial intelligence units or countries.

- Partnered with the financial intelligence unit in the United Arab Emirates to conduct a seminar on developing financial intelligence units for officials from Afghanistan, Bangladesh, Maldives, Pakistan and Sri Lanka.

- Worked with the financial intelligence unit in Mauritius to train analysts from India, Mauritius and South Africa in analytical and investigative methods related to money laundering.

For additional workload data, see Appendix D, Table D-7.

Priorities for Fiscal Year 2005

- Host the 13th Egmont Plenary in Washington, D.C. in June 2005. This will be a major international meeting requiring careful planning of program events and logistics, including physical and personnel security. At this meeting, Egmont membership is expected to grow to more than 100 financial intelligence units.

- Aggressively implement our international agenda, which will center on enhancing international liaison with financial intelligence units around the world and participating in numerous international groups that adopt and evaluate implementing measures to combat money laundering and terrorist financing. These include the Financial Action Task Force (FATF), and the global network of FATF-styled regional bodies: the Asia/Pacific Group on Money Laundering, the Caribbean Financial Action Task Force, the Council of Europe Select Committee of Experts on the Evaluation of Anti-Money Laundering Measures, the Eastern and Southern Africa Anti-Money Laundering Group; and the Financial Action Task Force on Money Laundering in South America. During 2005, we will also participate in two newly created FATF-style regional bodies, the Middle East and North Africa FATF and the Eurasia FATF.

"International terrorist groups need money to attract, support, and retain adherents throughout the world as well as to secure the loyalty of other groups that share the same goals. Thus, they need to devise schemes to raise, collect, and distribute money to operatives preparing for attacks. Their fundraising schemes and the movement of money internationally makes the terrorist funds vulnerable to detection if we have the right safeguards in place. It is now an accepted axiom worldwide that when you track and stop tainted money, you can dismantle international networks and save lives."

–Juan C. Zarate, Treasury Assistant Secretary, Office of Terrorist Financing and Financial Crime, Nov. 10, 2003

- Continue to provide training and technical support to enhance and establish financial intelligence units in various regions throughout the world. In 2005 priorities will center on South and South East Asia, the Middle East, and North Africa. Outreach will be made to the countries that have come together under the Eurasia FATF umbrella. In addition, FinCEN will continue its role in the "3 + 1" Working Group on terrorist financing in the Triborder Area, where Argentina, Brazil, and Paraguay converge. FinCEN expects to focus its resources on those countries that are most vulnerable to terrorist financing and to devise a strategy closely coordinated on an interagency basis to provide them with the necessary training and technical assistance to create comprehensive, effective anti-money laundering/anti-terrorist financing regimes.

- Step up personnel exchanges with a number of key allies on important complex cases and collaborate with Egmont members on strategic intelligence initiatives and transnational targeting efforts, including weapons of mass destruction and trafficking in women and children.

- Modernize the Egmont Secure Web system to leverage new technology, expand services to financial intelligence units, and facilitate information sharing.

Building the capacity of our coalition partners to combat money laundering and terrorist financing through cooperative efforts, and through training and technical assistance programs, is critical to our national security....The same measures that are required to establish a comprehensive anti-money laundering regime— sound legislation and regulations; suspicious transaction reporting mechanisms; financial intelligence units; on-site supervision of the financial sector; internal controls; trained financial investigators; legal authorization to utilize special investigative techniques; modern asset forfeiture and administrative blocking capability; and the ability to cooperate and share information internationally—are precisely the tools required to identify, interdict and disrupt terrorist financing.

–International Narcotics Control Strategy Report,
Bureau for International Narcotics and Law Enforcement Affairs,
Department of State, March 2004

5. Administration and Communications Division

As a steward of U.S. government resources funded by American taxpayers, the Financial Crimes Enforcement Network is committed to maintaining the highest standards of management excellence and integrity. The Division of Administration and Communication leads this effort by managing our financial resources; providing human resources leadership and services; ensuring staff training and individual development opportunities; developing publications and other channels for internal and external communications; and providing contracting, logistics, records management, and other essential services.

Major Accomplishments in Fiscal Year 2004

- Enhanced employee development by:

    - Establishing a new training function charged with developing career path progressions for all employees.

    - Providing training to 93 percent of FinCEN's employees. Some 75 percent of the training expenditures were for technical skills, and 14 percent of training expenditures were for executive, managerial, and supervisory training. The remainder were for equal employment opportunity and retirement planning training.

    - Opening new opportunities for employee learning by building partnerships with the Central Intelligence Agency's CIA University and CIA's Sherman Kent School for Intelligence Analysis, which provided opportunities for our analysts to be trained on economic, financial and trade issues with CIA analysts.

    - Narrowing gaps in technology skills by providing training in 39 areas related to information technology and software.

- Replaced a pass-fail employee performance rating system with a five-tier employee performance management system linked to the strategic plan.

- Prepared for or made the transition to new web-based financial and administrative services and systems, including time and attendance, travel, credit card, procurement, accounting, and business case management.

- Ensured management control systems provided reasonable assurance of compliance with the Federal Managers Financial Integrity Act. No material weaknesses were open in Fiscal Year 2004.

- Assumed human resource functions formerly provided by another agency in order to better manage all aspects related to human resources, including payroll.

- Helped increase public knowledge about the Financial Crimes Enforcement Network by:

  - Answering over 1,100 e-mails from the general public requesting information and/or assistance from FinCEN.

  - Responding to 151 requests for visits and/or speeches, and making arrangements for 57 visits and 55 speaking engagements within the Communications Division.

  - Publishing 16 press releases, including a statement from Director Fox on unauthorized disclosure of Suspicious Activity Reports.

- Assumed procurement functions formerly provided by other agencies and awarded the multi-year development and maintenance contract for BSA Direct, the new Bank Secrecy Act data storage and retrieval platform.

> *"I am proud of the accomplishments of the men and women of the Financial Crimes Enforcement Network.... These dedicated civil servants remain focused on the important and complex task of finding, following, and fracturing financial flows of money ... that support terror."*
>
> *–U.S. Senator Richard Shelby, Chair, U.S. Senate Committee on Banking, Housing, and Urban Affairs, April 29, 2004*

Priorities for Fiscal Year 2005

- Develop and implement a new performance recognition system to complement the new five-tier employee performance system.

- Design a comprehensive management training strategy in support of succession planning.

- Increase employee opportunities for learning in technology skills areas.

- Conduct an employee satisfaction survey and develop recommendations for areas where improvement needs are identified.

- Conduct the Office of Management and Budget's Program Assessment Rating Tool (PART) process. Conduct customer surveys to assist performance measurement processes and results.

- Evaluate new administrative processes and the financial and administrative systems adopted in FY 2004, and make any needed improvements.

- Update and improve the Financial Crimes Enforcement Network public website.

6. Office of Chief Counsel

The Financial Crimes Enforcement Network is dedicated to maintaining the highest legal and ethical standards of government service. The Office of Chief Counsel supports that goal by providing legal services to the bureau in the conduct of all its operations, ranging from statutory and regulatory interpretation and drafting to ethics determinations and training.

Major Accomplishments in Fiscal Year 2004

- Negotiated and drafted 28 memoranda of understanding with federal, state and local law enforcement and regulatory agencies for access to Bank Secrecy Act data and with Egmont partners for information sharing.

- Completed the new Redissemination Guidelines for Bank Secrecy Act data. The Guidelines set forth the terms and conditions under which federal, state and local agencies that access Bank Secrecy Act reports, electronically or otherwise, may further disseminate this sensitive information.

- Represented the Financial Crimes Enforcement Network on the Egmont Legal Working Group as Vice-Chair.

- Supported the Regulatory Policy and Programs Division by drafting Federal Register notices for rulemakings; reviewing and drafting regulatory rulings; and drafting penalty assessments.

- Supported the Office of Global Liaison by providing evaluations of anti-money laundering laws being developed by other countries.

- Provided ethics training for all Financial Crimes Enforcement Network employees.

For additional workload data, see Appendix D, Table D-8.

Priorities for Fiscal Year 2005

- Provide legal support to the Financial Crimes Enforcement Network's regulatory initiatives.

- Negotiate and draft memoranda of understanding with all requesting agencies authorized to exchange information with the Financial Crimes Enforcement Network.

33

- Continue to support the Egmont Legal Working Group in enhancing its processes.

- Complete a thorough review of contracting and procurement matters.

- Enhance employee ethics training with regular ethics releases.

"Perhaps the most fundamental ethical principle is that an employee undertakes a public trust. That trust means that employees should always serve the public interest….Whenever employees honor the public trust of their office, they fulfill the commitment that they make and earn the confidence of the American people."

–Marilyn L. Glynn, Acting Director, U.S. Office of Government Ethics, March 1, 2004

Appendix A:
Bank Secrecy Act Filings, by Type, Fiscal Year 2004

Type of Form[1]	Filed in FY 2003	Filed in FY 2004[2]	Percent e-filed in FY 2004
Currency Transaction Reports (all types)	13,341,699	13,674,114	11%
Suspicious Activity Reports (filed by all covered industries)	413,052	663,655	17%
Reports of Foreign Bank and Financial Accounts	199,738	218,667	0%
Registrations of Money Services Business	5,858	17,037	0%
Designations of Exempt Person	69,450	80,763	0%
Reports for Cash Payments Over $10,000 Received in a Trade or Business (Form 8300)	129,824	151,998	0%
Total	**14,159,621**	**14,806,234**	**11%**

[1] Figures for Reports of International Transportation of Currency or Monetary Instruments, which are collected by U.S. Customs and Border Protection, Department of Homeland Security, are not included.

[2] Figures as of January 6, 2005.

For copies of the latest versions of these forms, see the FinCEN website at **www.fincen.gov/reg_bsaforms.html.**

(August 29, 2004)

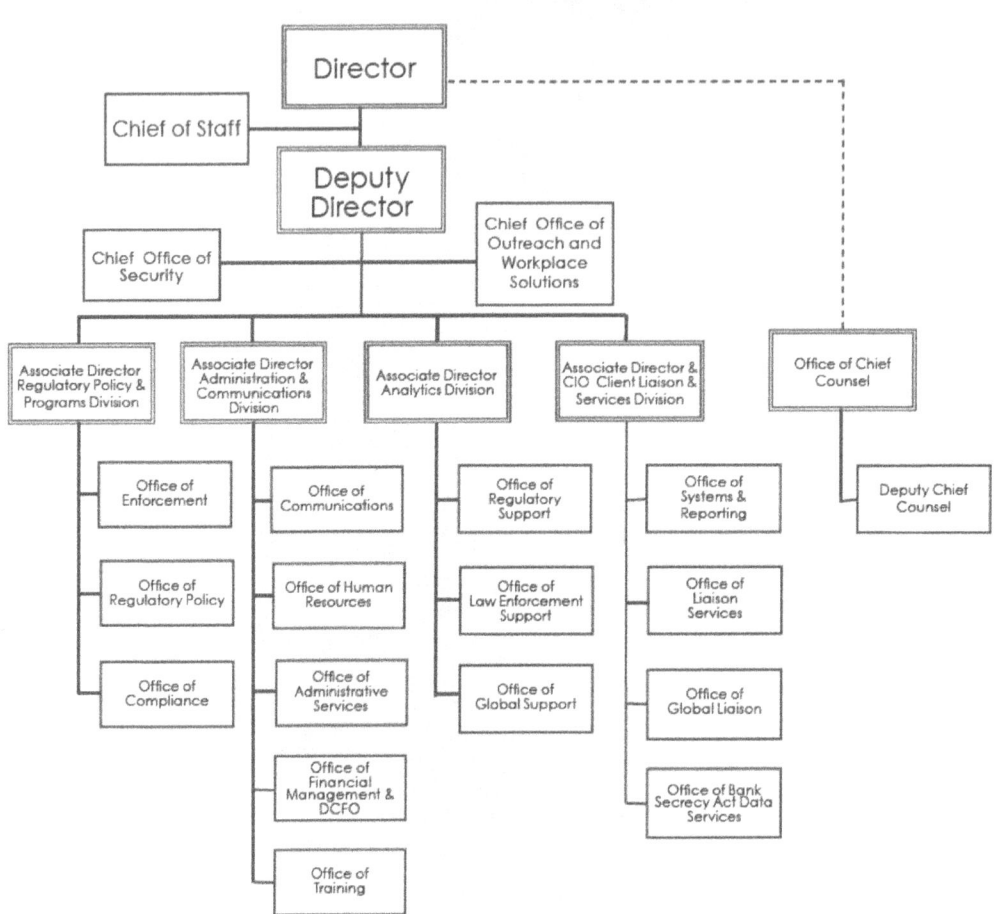

Appendix C: Key Officials

William J. Fox
Director

William J. Fox was appointed the fourth Director of the Financial Crimes Enforcement Network on December 1, 2003. Prior to his appointment, Mr. Fox served as Treasury's Associate Deputy General Counsel and Acting Deputy General Counsel. After September 11, 2001, he also served as the principal assistant and senior advisor to Treasury's General Counsel on issues relating to terrorist financing and financial crime.

Mr. Fox joined the Department of the Treasury in December 2000 as the Acting Deputy Assistant General Counsel for Enforcement. From 1988 to December 2000, he served at the Bureau of Alcohol, Tobacco and Firearms (ATF), first as an attorney in ATF's Chicago office, then as the Senior Counsel for Alcohol and Tobacco and finally as ATF's Deputy Chief Counsel. During his time with ATF, Mr. Fox provided legal support to several large scale criminal investigations; helped oversee ATF's regulatory program; served as a legal point person for ATF's alcohol and tobacco diversion program; worked on several important legislative initiatives; and, served as principal legal support for the United States Trade Representative's Office for wine trade negotiations.

Mr. Fox was born and raised in Nebraska. He received his Bachelor's degree in History and his Law degree from Creighton University in Omaha.

William F. Baity
Deputy Director

William F. Baity was appointed Deputy Director of the Financial Crimes Enforcement Network (FinCEN) in January 1995. As Deputy Director, Mr. Baity is responsible for working with the law enforcement, financial and regulatory communities to insure the effective coordination of anti-money laundering initiatives. He has also been elected to Chair the Egmont Committee of the Egmont Group, currently consisting of financial intelligence units from 94 countries with the goal of providing a forum for improving information sharing and support to their respective governments in the fight against money laundering, terrorist financing, and other financial crimes.

Before joining FinCEN, Mr. Baity served as Acting Director, Deputy Director, and a U.S. Trustee for the United States Bankruptcy Trustee Program of the Department of Justice. He also held positions as Assistant United States Attorney, Assistant Director Legal Officer in the United States Coast Guard, and Special Assistant U.S. Attorney. Before joining the Government, he worked for the Exxon Company as an Economic and Business Analyst.

Mr. Baity received a Bachelor's Degree in mathematics from North Carolina College, a Master's Degree in industrial administration from Carnegie-Mellon University, and a J.D. from Vanderbilt University. He is admitted to the Bars of the States of Louisiana and Tennessee.

Jack Cunniff
Associate Director/CIO, Client Liaison & Services

Jack Cunniff oversees FinCEN's information technology and liaison initiatives in support of our partners within the law enforcement, regulatory and international communities. He came to FinCEN in December 2003 as the Gateway Program Manager. Prior to arriving at FinCEN, Mr. Cunniff was the Deputy Assistant Inspector General for Investigations at the Federal Emergency Management Agency, Office of Inspector General. That office became the Department of Homeland Security Office of Inspector General. Prior to this position, Mr. Cunniff served as a Senior Policy Advisor for the Under Secretary of Treasury (Enforcement).

Mr. Cunniff began his law enforcement career as a Special Agent with the Secret Service in New York in 1975. He held senior management positions in the Intelligence and Presidential Protective Divisions, ending his career with the Secret Service in 1999 as the Special Agent in Charge of the Office of Protective Operations. Mr. Cunniff received his bachelor's degree from Northeastern University in Boston.

William D. Langford
Associate Director, Regulatory Policy and Programs

William D. Langford joined FinCEN in January 2004 as a principal advisor to the Director for strategic development and administration of regulations involving the Bank Secrecy Act. He previously served as Senior Advisor to the General Counsel of the Department of Treasury. Since September 11, his focus has been largely on the implementation of the anti-terrorism and anti-money laundering provisions of the USA PATRIOT Act, including the drafting of the regulations implementing these provisions.

Previously, Mr. Langford served as Senior Counsel for Financial Crimes in the Office of the Assistant General Counsel for Enforcement of the Department of the Treasury. He holds a Bachelor of Arts degree in mathematics from Hastings College in Nebraska, and a J.D. from the University of Texas School of Law.

David M. Vogt
Associate Director, Analytics

David M. Vogt directs FinCEN's Division of Analytics, which conducts policy-level financial and threat analyses, as well as analyses in support of domestic law enforcement investigations, international law enforcement investigations, regulatory activities, and intelligence agencies. Before assuming his current post, Mr. Vogt served as FinCEN's Strategic Planning Advisor. As a member of the bureau's senior management team, he was responsible for developing plans and strategies for the implementation and integration of program initiatives across FinCEN organizational lines.

Since joining FinCEN at its inception in 1990, he has served as Acting Deputy Director and as an Assistant or Associate Director in each of the bureau's primary operational areas. Mr. Vogt's extensive experience before joining FinCEN included serving as a civilian employee in various capacities at the National Security Agency from 1975-1988. He received Bachelor of Arts and Masters degrees from the University of Missouri.

Diane K. Wade
Associate Director, Administration &Communications

Diane K. Wade directs FinCEN's Administration and Communications Division, which provides human resources, financial management, administrative, and communications services for the bureau. Before joining FinCEN, Ms. Wade led a team implementing the Department of Energy's Budget and Performance Integration and Five-Year planning initiatives.

Prior to serving at Energy, Ms. Wade was a civilian employee in the Department of the Army, serving most recently as Acting Deputy Division Chief, Operating Force Division, in the Army's Budget Office. In that position she was responsible for the formulation and justification of the Army's $21.0 billion dollar operations budget. Ms. Wade also led the preparation and justification of the Army's Training and Mobilization budgets and served as Chief, Resource Management Division, of the Army's Material Command - Far East. She holds a Bachelor of Science degree in marketing from George Mason University in Virginia.

Appendix D: Key Workload Statistics

Table D-1: Regulatory Activity	FY 2003	FY 2004
Number of industries covered by Anti-Money Laundering Program requirements	8	10[1]
Number of industries with Suspicious Activity Reporting requirements	7	8[2]
Number of special measures instituted under Sectionc311 of USA PATRIOT Act	0	3
Number of regulatory inquiries answered (telephone, written, e-mail, and publication requests)	7,119	8,893
Number of calls to Financial Institutions Hotline, on which institutions report suspicious activities that may indicate terrorism	296	297
Number of federal and state financial regulators with whom Memoranda of Understanding have been executed	0	5
Number of compliance matters referred to FinCEN for possible enforcement action	49	52
Amount of civil penalties assessed	$24.3 million	$25.01 million
Number of rulings issued interpreting Bank Secrecy Act regulations concerning money services businesses	8	7
Bank Secrecy Act forms revised	8[3]	4[4]
Bank Secrecy Act forms for which revisions were proposed	3[5]	1[6]

[1] Banks, thrifts, credit unions, casinos, money services businesses, securities broker-dealers, introducing brokers, credit card system operators, mutual funds, and futures commission merchants

[2] Banks, thrifts, credit unions, casinos, money services businesses, securities broker-dealers, introducing brokers, and futures commission merchants

[3] Suspicious Activity Report-Securities/Futures; Suspicious Activity Report-Money Services Business; Suspicious Activity Report-Depository Institution; Suspicious Activity Report-Casino; Report of International Transportation of Currency or Monetary Instruments; Currency Transaction Report Casinos- Nevada; Currency Transaction Report; Currency Transaction Report for Trade or Business (Form 8300)

[4] Currency Transaction Report; Suspicious Activity Report-Securities/Futures; Money Services Business Registration; Designation of Exempt Person

[5] Suspicous Activity Report –Securities/Futures; Suspicious Activity Report-Depository Institution; Suspicious Activity Report-Casino

[6] Report of International Transportation of Currency or Monetary Instruments

Table D-2: Analytic Products	FY 2003	FY 2004
Analytic products completed by FinCEN employees and contractors to support law enforcement investigations	4,403	2,913
Number of subjects researched by FinCEN employees and contractors	30,429	19,304
Number of analytical products to support intelligence community	175	79
Number of proactive analyses initiated by FinCEN and referred to law enforcement	249	266
Number of potential investigative subjects identified through proactive analyses initiated by FinCEN	2,197	2,874
Number of analytical products related to geographic threat assessments, money laundering/illicit financing methodologies, and/or analysis of Bank Secrecy Act compliance patterns	79	56
Number of law enforcement cases supported through information exchanges with foreign jurisdictions	724	844

Table D-3: Law Enforcement Support	FY 2003	FY 2004
Number of law enforcement cases supported through research by FinCEN and/or through access provided by FinCEN to Bank Secrecy Act data (includes cases researched by employees, contractors, Platform/detailees, and Gateway users)	15,871	20,349
Number of subjects researched for law enforcement by FinCEN and by law enforcement agencies accessing Bank Secrecy Act data through FinCEN (includes subjects in all cases cited above)	61,753	62,683
Total cases networked with other law enforcement agencies investigating same subject(s)	3,540	5,466

Table D-4: Gateway Program	FY 2003	FY 2004
Number of Gateway users	1,105	2,181
Number of Gateway cases	9,410	14,795
Number of subjects identified in Gateway cases	22,980	33,954
Gateway alerts[1]	2,927	5,542
Gateway Commercial Database Requests	4,749	5,219
Gateway inspections	30	313
Gateway users trained	1,053	1,007

[1] *Alerts are indications that subjects researched in the Bank Secrecy Act database by Gateway users have been researched by other users and/or appear in law enforcement databases queried by FinCEN.*

Table D-5: Platform Program	FY 2003	FY 2004
Number of cases supported	2,058	2,640
Number of subjects identified in Platform cases	8,345	9,425

Table D-6: Law Enforcement-Financial Institution Information Sharing Program (314 Program)	FY 2003	FY 2004
Number of information requests received from law enforcement agencies for submission to financial institutions under the Law Enforcement-Financial Institution Information Sharing program authorized by Section 314(a) of USA PATRIOT Act	159	255
Number of vetted 314(a) requests involving terrorism, money laundering, or both sent out to financial institution points of contact	147	198
Number of subjects named in requests	1,089	1,501
Number of financial institution points of contact for information exchanges (last transmission of year)	31,445	35,179
Number of responses received from financial institutions	6,516	11,699

Table D-7: Global Activity	FY 2003	FY 2004
Number of countries to which Financial Crimes Enforcement Network provided assistance in establishing financial intelligence units	9	11
Number of established financial intelligence units to which Financial Crimes Enforcement Network provided regulatory and technical assistance	34	27
Number of financial intelligence units connected to Egmont Secure Web during fiscal year	13 (64 were connected)	21 (85 are now connected)

Table D-8: Office of Chief Counsel Activity	FY 2003	FY 2004
Regulations and Federal Register Notices issued	47	28
Advisories issued	8	5
Memoranda of Understanding completed	11	28
Regulatory rulings issued	0	3
Enforcement actions	4	4

Appendix E: Key Internal Activity

Staffing, as of September 30, 2004	
Employees on board	249 plus 4 students
Employees by job title	Intelligence Research Specialists – 107 Program & Administrative Staff – 49 Information Technology Specialists – 29 Inspection and Investigative Specialists – 12 Attorneys – 10 Other – 42
Managers	Senior Executive Service – 4 Other Managers – 22 Nonsupervisory Employees – 223, plus 4 students
Vacancies in FY 2004	Posted – 65 Filled – 33 Selections made and in process – 12 Remainder – 20 (selections not yet made or posting cancelled)

Internal Security Activity, FY 2004	
Number of employees and contractors provided security awareness training	133
Security reports/surveys completed[1]	2
Information systems fully certified and accredited (C&A) as secure during the year[2]	1
Proportion of major systems with security C&A	100%

[1] Completed reports were the Annual Accounting of Classified Documents Report and the Classified Survey of Federal Explosives Detection Assets.

[2] The system for e-filing Bank Secrecy Act reports was fully certified and accredited.

Financial Crimes Enforcement Network Diversity Profile, September 30, 2004			
	Male	**Female**	**Total**
Total employees	43.3%	56.7%	100%
Hispanic/Latino	1.2%	2.0%	3.2%
White	33.1%	37.0%	70.1%
Black/African American	5.9%	14.6%	20.5%
American Indian/ Alaska Native	0%	.8%	.8%
Asian	3.1%	2.4%	5.5%
Employees with Disabilities	2.4%	3.5%	5.9%

Equal Employment and Diversity Activity, FY 2004	
Special Emphasis Programs presented addressing gender, ethnic and health issues in the workplace	4
Other programs coordinated/sponsored[1]	3
Studies completed[2]	1
Partnerships established [3]	1
Informal Equal Employment Opportunity complaints resolved	6
Formal Equal Employment Opportunity complaints filed	2

[1]Programs included FinCEN Diversity Day; Bring Your Child to Work Day; and Leadership Session on Recruitment, Training, Mentoring, and Adopt a School Initiatives.

[2] Workplace Accessibility Study was completed.

[3] A partnership was established with the Hispanic Association of Colleges and Universities.

Appendix F: Financial Information

Financial Crimes Enforcement Network – Direct Obligations, Fiscal Years 2003 and 2004, by Object Classification

(dollars in thousands)

Object Classification	FY 2004 Actual	FY 2003 Actual
Personnel compensation:		
Permanent positions	$ 20,539	$17,449
Positions other than permanent	284	468
Other personnel compensation	526	448
Special personal services payments	-	-
Total personnel compensation	**$ 21,349**	**$ 18,365**
Civilian personnel benefits	4,947	4,127
Benefits to former personnel	-	-
Travel and transportation of persons	796	663
Rents, communications and utilities:		
Rental payments to GSA	2,076	3,010
Rental payments to others	42	43
Other rents, communications and utilities	769	550
Printing and reproduction	200	1,061
Other services:		
Advisory & assistance services	773	472
Other services	4,009	3,015
Purchase of goods/services from Government accounts	9,956	6,549
Operation & maintenance of facilities	2,566	708
Medical care	107	94
Operation & maintenance of equipment	6,480	6,104
Supplies and materials	335	321
Equipment	1,475	2,533
Insurance claims and indemnities	-	5
Total obligations	**$ 55,880**	**$ 47,620**
Change in unobligated balance from prior year	1,351	3,796
Total enacted appropriations and budget estimate	**$ 57,231**	**$ 51,416**

History of President's Budget Requests, Appropriations, and Obligations, FY 2002 – 2004
(dollars in thousands)

	FY 2002	FY 2003	FY 2004
President's Budget Request	$45,155	$50,517	$57,571
Final Appropriated Enacted Level	$47,537	$51,416	$57,231
Unobligated Balance Lapsing	$114	$206	$252

Fiscal Year 2004
Financial Performance Indicators

Financial Area	Treasury Standard for "Green"[1]	FinCEN FY 2004 Average	FinCEN Score
% of cash reconciled to total	>99.99%	100%	Green
% of uncleared suspense transactions over 60 days	<10%	0%	Green
% of Accounts Receivable from public delinquent over180 days	<10%	99%	Red[2]
% of electronic vendor payments	96%	90%	Yellow
% non-credit card invoices paid on time	>98%	95%	Red[3]
% of centrally billed travel cards with balances over 61 days past due	0%	0%	Green
% of individually billed travel cards with balances over 61 days past due	<2%	.65%	Green
% of purchase cards with balances over 61 days past due	0%	0%	Green

[1] The Treasury Department sets standards for Green, Yellow, and Red performance. Only standards for Green are shown in this table.

[2] The benchmark for red is 20% of accounts receivable from the public delinquent over 180 days. In the normal course of business, FinCEN does not incur large accounts receivable from the public. These receivables include two civil monetary penalties dating from FY 2001 that were referred for collection in April 2002. Although collection efforts will continue on this debt, we are required to write off all delinquent debt older than two years and place in 'Currently Not Collectible Account'. The principal, with accrued interest, was written off in late FY 2004 and early FY 2005.

[3] The benchmark for red is less than 97% of non-credit card invoices paid on time. FinCEN paid 917 invoices in FY 2004, 51 of which were paid late. The majority of late payments occurred due to the transition to new financial systems and a new accounting cross-service provider. Corrective actions have been taken.

Appendix G: Program Evaluations

The Financial Crimes Enforcement Network relies on internal and external program evaluations to gauge program effectiveness and make improvements as needed. Listed below are key evaluations completed and underway during FY 2004.

Government Accountability Office Audits

Completed in FY 2004:
- GAO-04-163, Terrorist Financing: U.S. Agencies Should Systematically Assess Terrorists' Use of Alternative Financing Mechanisms

Underway in FY 2004:
- Implementation of Sections 326 and 314 of the USA PATRIOT Act
- Effectiveness of Bank Secrecy Act Examinations and Enforcement

Treasury Office of Inspector General Audits

Underway in FY 2004:
- Analysis and Dissemination of Bank Secrecy Act and Criminal Data
- Electronic Filing of Bank Secrecy Act Reports
- FinCEN Reliability of Suspicious Activity Reports (Follow-up)
- FinCEN Registration of Money Services Businesses

Internal Control Reviews and Program Evaluations

Completed in FY 2004:
- Internal Control Review of FinCEN's Purchase Card Program
- Internal Control Review of FinCEN's Promotional Items and Gifts
- Evaluation of Office of Investigative Support Work Processes
- Evaluation of Goods Receipt Processing and Information Technology Inventory Control

Appendix H: Oversight Agencies

The Financial Crimes Enforcement Network reports to the Department of the Treasury's Office of Terrorism and Financial Intelligence. The following Congressional and Senate Committees and Subcommittees have authorizing and appropriations responsibilities for our operations.

U.S. House of Representatives Committees

- Committee on Financial Services, Subcommittee on Oversight and Investigations (Authorizing Committee)

- Committee on Appropriations, Subcommittee on Transportation, Treasury and Independent Agencies (Appropriating Committee)

U.S. Senate Committees

- Committee on Banking, Housing, and Urban Affairs (Authorizing Committee)

- Committee on Appropriations, Subcommittee on Transportation, Treasury and General Government (Appropriating Committee)

"Since its establishment in 1990, FinCEN has been a service-oriented, information sharing agency dedicated to collecting, analyzing and disseminating financial data to help identify and trace the financial intersection of potential criminal and terrorist activity. While FinCEN is a small agency with relatively little funding, the agency is at the center of our nation's anti-money laundering infrastructure, supporting the crucial work of the financial services, law enforcement and intelligence communities."

–Memo to Colleagues from six U.S. Representatives, September 14, 2004

www.ingramcontent.com/pod-product-compliance
Lightning Source LLC
Chambersburg PA
CBHW08055290526
45790CB00006B/2661